50 Easy Summer BBQ Recipes for Home

By: Kelly Johnson

Table of Contents

- Grilled BBQ Ribs
- BBQ Chicken Skewers
- Grilled Veggie Platter
- Classic Cheeseburgers
- BBQ Pulled Pork Sandwiches
- Grilled Corn on the Cob
- Teriyaki Chicken Thighs
- Smoked Brisket
- BBQ Shrimp Skewers
- Grilled Sausages with Peppers
- Sweet and Spicy BBQ Chicken
- Grilled Portobello Mushrooms
- BBQ Beef Kebabs
- Grilled Pineapple with Honey Glaze
- BBQ Fish Tacos
- Smoked Chicken Wings
- Grilled Zucchini with Parmesan
- BBQ Meatball Skewers
- Spicy Grilled Shrimp
- Grilled Asparagus with Lemon
- BBQ Pulled Chicken Sliders
- Grilled Peach Salad with Balsamic Glaze
- BBQ Lamb Chops
- Sweet Potato Fries
- Grilled Flatbreads with Toppings
- BBQ Chicken Caesar Salad
- Grilled Beef Tenderloin
- Roasted Garlic and Herb Chicken
- BBQ Duck Breast
- Grilled Caprese Skewers
- Sweet BBQ Glazed Baby Carrots
- BBQ Sliced Brisket Tacos
- Grilled Bacon-Wrapped Jalapeños
- BBQ Veggie Skewers
- Grilled Flat Iron Steak

- Roasted Corn and Black Bean Salad
- BBQ Beef Short Ribs
- Grilled Fajita Veggies
- BBQ Sausage and Peppers Sandwiches
- Grilled Avocados with Salsa
- BBQ Grilled Chicken Wraps
- Grilled Clams with Garlic Butter
- BBQ Smoked Sausages with Sauerkraut
- Grilled BBQ Sliders
- BBQ Grilled Fish Fillets
- Grilled Stuffed Bell Peppers
- BBQ Brisket Nachos
- Grilled Eggplant with Tahini Sauce
- Grilled BBQ Chicken Pizza
- Grilled Watermelon with Mint

Grilled BBQ Ribs

Ingredients:

- 2 racks of baby back ribs
- 2 tablespoons olive oil
- **Salt and pepper** (to taste)
- **1 cup BBQ sauce** (your choice of brand or homemade)

For the dry rub:

- 2 tablespoons brown sugar
- 1 tablespoon paprika
- 1 tablespoon garlic powder
- 1 tablespoon onion powder
- 1 tablespoon ground cumin
- 1 tablespoon chili powder
- 1 teaspoon cayenne pepper (optional for heat)
- 1 teaspoon black pepper
- 1 teaspoon salt

Instructions:

1. **Prep the ribs**:
   - Remove the membrane from the back of the ribs by gently lifting it with a knife and pulling it off.
   - Rub the ribs with olive oil, then generously season them with salt and pepper.
2. **Make the dry rub**:
   - In a small bowl, mix together all the ingredients for the dry rub. Sprinkle the rub evenly over both sides of the ribs, patting it in gently.
3. **Preheat the grill**:
   - Preheat your grill to medium heat, around 300°F (150°C). You'll be grilling with indirect heat, so only one side of the grill should be turned on.
4. **Grill the ribs**:
   - Place the ribs on the grill, bone side down, over the cooler side of the grill (indirect heat).
   - Close the lid and cook the ribs for 2.5 to 3 hours, turning them occasionally. The ribs should be tender and cooked through.
5. **Add BBQ sauce**:

- In the last 20 minutes of grilling, brush your favorite BBQ sauce over the ribs. Continue to grill, turning occasionally and adding more sauce as you go, until the sauce caramelizes.
6. **Serve**:
    - Once the ribs are tender and the sauce is beautifully glazed, remove them from the grill.
    - Let the ribs rest for a few minutes, then slice and serve hot with extra BBQ sauce on the side.

BBQ Chicken Skewers

Ingredients:

- **4 boneless chicken breasts**, cut into 1-inch cubes
- **1/2 cup BBQ sauce**
- **1 tablespoon olive oil**
- **Salt and pepper** (to taste)
- **Wooden skewers** (soaked in water for 30 minutes)

Instructions:

1. Preheat grill to medium-high heat.
2. Thread the chicken cubes onto skewers.
3. Brush the chicken with olive oil and season with salt and pepper.
4. Grill the skewers for 5-7 minutes on each side until fully cooked, brushing with BBQ sauce during the last few minutes.
5. Serve with extra BBQ sauce on the side.

Grilled Veggie Platter

Ingredients:

- **2 zucchinis**, sliced into rounds
- **2 bell peppers**, cut into strips
- **1 red onion**, cut into wedges
- **1 cup cherry tomatoes**
- **1 tablespoon olive oil**
- **Salt and pepper** (to taste)
- **1 teaspoon dried oregano**

Instructions:

1. Preheat the grill to medium-high heat.
2. Toss the vegetables in olive oil, salt, pepper, and oregano.
3. Grill the veggies for 3-5 minutes per side, or until they are tender and slightly charred.
4. Serve on a platter with a drizzle of balsamic glaze or lemon juice.

Classic Cheeseburgers

Ingredients:

- **1 lb ground beef** (80% lean)
- **Salt and pepper** (to taste)
- **4 hamburger buns**
- **4 slices of cheddar cheese**
- **Lettuce, tomato, onions** (optional toppings)
- **Ketchup, mustard, pickles** (optional condiments)

Instructions:

1. Preheat the grill to medium-high heat.
2. Form the ground beef into 4 equal patties. Season both sides with salt and pepper.
3. Grill the patties for about 4-5 minutes on each side, until cooked through.
4. Place a slice of cheese on each patty during the last minute of grilling.
5. Toast the buns on the grill for 1-2 minutes.
6. Assemble the burgers with your favorite toppings and condiments.

BBQ Pulled Pork Sandwiches

Ingredients:

- **2 lb pork shoulder**
- **1 cup BBQ sauce**
- **1 tablespoon olive oil**
- **Salt and pepper** (to taste)
- **4 hamburger buns**
- **Coleslaw** (optional topping)

Instructions:

1. Preheat grill to medium heat.
2. Season the pork shoulder with olive oil, salt, and pepper.
3. Grill the pork for 1.5-2 hours, turning occasionally until the internal temperature reaches 190°F (88°C).
4. Shred the pork using two forks and mix with BBQ sauce.
5. Serve on toasted buns with coleslaw, if desired.

Grilled Corn on the Cob

Ingredients:

- **4 ears of corn**, husked
- **2 tablespoons butter**
- **Salt and pepper** (to taste)
- **1 teaspoon paprika** (optional)

Instructions:

1. Preheat grill to medium-high heat.
2. Place the corn directly on the grill, turning occasionally, for 10-12 minutes until charred and tender.
3. Brush with butter and season with salt, pepper, and paprika.
4. Serve immediately.

Teriyaki Chicken Thighs

Ingredients:

- 4 bone-in chicken thighs
- 1/2 cup teriyaki sauce
- 1 tablespoon honey
- 2 cloves garlic, minced
- 1 tablespoon sesame oil

Instructions:

1. Preheat grill to medium-high heat.
2. Mix the teriyaki sauce, honey, garlic, and sesame oil.
3. Marinate the chicken thighs in the sauce mixture for 30 minutes.
4. Grill the chicken for 6-8 minutes per side, until cooked through, brushing with more marinade during grilling.
5. Serve with rice or vegetables.

Smoked Brisket

Ingredients:

- 4 lb beef brisket
- 2 tablespoons olive oil
- 1 tablespoon salt
- 1 tablespoon black pepper
- 1 tablespoon paprika
- 1 tablespoon garlic powder
- 1 tablespoon onion powder

Instructions:

1. Preheat smoker to 225°F (107°C).
2. Rub the brisket with olive oil and season with salt, pepper, paprika, garlic powder, and onion powder.
3. Place the brisket in the smoker and cook for 10-12 hours, until the internal temperature reaches 190°F (88°C).
4. Let the brisket rest for 30 minutes before slicing and serving.

BBQ Shrimp Skewers

Ingredients:

- **1 lb large shrimp**, peeled and deveined
- **1/4 cup BBQ sauce**
- **1 tablespoon olive oil**
- **1 tablespoon lemon juice**
- **Wooden skewers**, soaked in water

Instructions:

1. Preheat the grill to medium-high heat.
2. In a bowl, mix BBQ sauce, olive oil, and lemon juice.
3. Thread the shrimp onto the skewers and brush with the BBQ sauce mixture.
4. Grill for 2-3 minutes per side, until the shrimp are cooked through and slightly charred.
5. Serve with extra BBQ sauce on the side.

Grilled Sausages with Peppers

Ingredients:

- **4 sausages** (your choice of flavor)
- **2 bell peppers**, sliced
- **1 large onion**, sliced
- **1 tablespoon olive oil**
- **Salt and pepper** (to taste)
- **1 teaspoon dried oregano**

Instructions:

1. Preheat grill to medium-high heat.
2. Brush the sausages with olive oil and season with salt, pepper, and oregano.
3. Grill sausages for 5-7 minutes per side, or until cooked through.
4. While the sausages cook, toss the peppers and onions in olive oil, salt, and pepper.
5. Grill the peppers and onions for 4-5 minutes until tender.
6. Serve the sausages with grilled peppers and onions.

Sweet and Spicy BBQ Chicken

Ingredients:

- **4 boneless, skinless chicken breasts**
- **1/4 cup BBQ sauce**
- **2 tablespoons honey**
- **1 tablespoon sriracha or hot sauce** (optional for heat)
- **1 tablespoon olive oil**
- **Salt and pepper** (to taste)

Instructions:

1. Preheat the grill to medium-high heat.
2. In a small bowl, mix BBQ sauce, honey, sriracha, olive oil, salt, and pepper.
3. Brush the chicken breasts with the sauce mixture.
4. Grill the chicken for 5-7 minutes on each side, until cooked through, brushing with more sauce as it grills.
5. Serve hot, garnished with extra sauce if desired.

Grilled Portobello Mushrooms

Ingredients:

- 4 large portobello mushroom caps
- 2 tablespoons olive oil
- 1 tablespoon balsamic vinegar
- **2 cloves garlic**, minced
- **Salt and pepper** (to taste)
- **1 teaspoon fresh thyme** (optional)

Instructions:

1. Preheat grill to medium-high heat.
2. Remove the stems from the mushrooms and clean the caps.
3. Mix olive oil, balsamic vinegar, garlic, salt, and pepper in a small bowl.
4. Brush the mushroom caps with the mixture and season with thyme.
5. Grill the mushrooms for 4-5 minutes on each side, until tender.
6. Serve as a side dish or on buns as a vegetarian burger.

BBQ Beef Kebabs

Ingredients:

- **1 lb beef sirloin**, cut into 1-inch cubes
- **1 bell pepper**, cut into 1-inch pieces
- **1 red onion**, cut into wedges
- **1 zucchini**, sliced
- **1/4 cup olive oil**
- **2 tablespoons soy sauce**
- **1 tablespoon Worcestershire sauce**
- **1 tablespoon garlic powder**
- **Salt and pepper** (to taste)
- **Wooden skewers** (soaked in water for 30 minutes)

Instructions:

1. Preheat grill to medium-high heat.
2. In a bowl, combine olive oil, soy sauce, Worcestershire sauce, garlic powder, salt, and pepper.
3. Thread the beef, bell pepper, onion, and zucchini onto the skewers, alternating the ingredients.
4. Brush the skewers with the marinade and grill for 5-7 minutes on each side, or until beef is cooked to desired doneness.
5. Serve with a side of rice or grilled vegetables.

Grilled Pineapple with Honey Glaze

Ingredients:

- **1 pineapple**, peeled and sliced into rings
- **2 tablespoons honey**
- **1 tablespoon lime juice**
- **1/2 teaspoon ground cinnamon** (optional)

Instructions:

1. Preheat grill to medium heat.
2. Mix honey, lime juice, and cinnamon (if using) in a small bowl.
3. Brush the pineapple slices with the honey glaze.
4. Grill the pineapple slices for 2-3 minutes on each side, until caramelized and grill marks appear.
5. Serve warm as a dessert or side dish.

BBQ Fish Tacos

Ingredients:

- **4 white fish fillets** (such as tilapia or mahi-mahi)
- **1 tablespoon olive oil**
- **1 tablespoon lime juice**
- **1 teaspoon chili powder**
- **Salt and pepper** (to taste)
- **4 small tortillas**
- **Shredded cabbage** (for topping)
- **Fresh cilantro** (for garnish)
- **Sour cream or salsa** (optional)

Instructions:

1. Preheat grill to medium-high heat.
2. Brush fish fillets with olive oil, lime juice, chili powder, salt, and pepper.
3. Grill the fish for 3-4 minutes per side until cooked through and easily flakes with a fork.
4. Warm tortillas on the grill for 1-2 minutes.
5. Assemble the tacos by placing the grilled fish on tortillas and topping with shredded cabbage, cilantro, and optional sour cream or salsa.

Smoked Chicken Wings

Ingredients:

- **12 chicken wings**
- **2 tablespoons olive oil**
- **1/4 cup BBQ sauce**
- **Salt and pepper** (to taste)
- **Wood chips** (for smoking)

Instructions:

1. Preheat smoker to 225°F (107°C) and prepare wood chips.
2. Coat the chicken wings with olive oil, salt, and pepper.
3. Place wings in the smoker and cook for 2-2.5 hours, until the internal temperature reaches 165°F (74°C).
4. In the last 10 minutes, brush the wings with BBQ sauce.
5. Serve with extra sauce and dipping sides like celery or carrots.

Grilled Zucchini with Parmesan

Ingredients:

- **2 zucchinis**, sliced into rounds or strips
- **1 tablespoon olive oil**
- **Salt and pepper** (to taste)
- **1/4 cup grated Parmesan cheese**
- **1 tablespoon fresh basil** (optional)

Instructions:

1. Preheat grill to medium heat.
2. Toss zucchini slices in olive oil, salt, and pepper.
3. Grill the zucchini for 2-3 minutes per side until tender and lightly charred.
4. Sprinkle with Parmesan cheese and fresh basil.
5. Serve warm as a side dish.

BBQ Meatball Skewers

Ingredients:

- 1 lb ground beef or turkey
- 1/4 cup breadcrumbs
- 1/4 cup grated Parmesan cheese
- 1 egg
- **2 cloves garlic**, minced
- **1 tablespoon Italian seasoning**
- **Salt and pepper** (to taste)
- **1/2 cup BBQ sauce**
- **Wooden skewers** (soaked in water for 30 minutes)

Instructions:

1. Preheat grill to medium-high heat.
2. In a bowl, combine the ground meat, breadcrumbs, Parmesan, egg, garlic, Italian seasoning, salt, and pepper. Mix until well combined.
3. Form the mixture into 1-inch meatballs and thread them onto skewers.
4. Grill the meatballs for 5-7 minutes on each side, until cooked through.
5. Brush with BBQ sauce during the last few minutes of grilling.
6. Serve with extra BBQ sauce on the side.

Spicy Grilled Shrimp

Ingredients:

- **1 lb large shrimp**, peeled and deveined
- **2 tablespoons olive oil**
- **2 tablespoons sriracha or hot sauce**
- **1 tablespoon lime juice**
- **2 cloves garlic**, minced
- **Salt and pepper** (to taste)

Instructions:

1. Preheat grill to medium-high heat.
2. In a bowl, combine olive oil, sriracha, lime juice, garlic, salt, and pepper.
3. Toss the shrimp in the sauce mixture and let marinate for 10-15 minutes.
4. Thread shrimp onto skewers and grill for 2-3 minutes per side, until cooked through.
5. Serve with a squeeze of lime and extra hot sauce if desired.

Grilled Asparagus with Lemon

Ingredients:

- **1 bunch asparagus**, trimmed
- **2 tablespoons olive oil**
- **Salt and pepper** (to taste)
- **1 lemon**, thinly sliced

Instructions:

1. Preheat grill to medium-high heat.
2. Toss the asparagus in olive oil and season with salt and pepper.
3. Grill the asparagus for 4-5 minutes, turning occasionally, until tender and charred.
4. Serve with a squeeze of lemon juice and lemon slices.

BBQ Pulled Chicken Sliders

Ingredients:

- **4 boneless, skinless chicken breasts**
- **1 cup BBQ sauce**
- **1 tablespoon olive oil**
- **Salt and pepper** (to taste)
- **Mini slider buns**
- **Coleslaw** (optional topping)

Instructions:

1. Preheat grill to medium-high heat.
2. Season the chicken breasts with olive oil, salt, and pepper.
3. Grill the chicken for 6-7 minutes on each side, until cooked through.
4. Shred the chicken using two forks and mix with BBQ sauce.
5. Serve on mini slider buns with coleslaw on top, if desired.

Grilled Peach Salad with Balsamic Glaze

Ingredients:

- **2 ripe peaches**, sliced
- **4 cups mixed greens**
- **1/4 cup crumbled goat cheese**
- **1/4 cup walnuts**, toasted
- **1 tablespoon olive oil**
- **Salt and pepper** (to taste)
- **Balsamic glaze** (for drizzling)

Instructions:

1. Preheat grill to medium heat.
2. Toss peach slices in olive oil, salt, and pepper.
3. Grill peaches for 2-3 minutes per side until slightly charred and softened.
4. Toss mixed greens with goat cheese and walnuts.
5. Arrange the grilled peaches on top and drizzle with balsamic glaze before serving.

BBQ Lamb Chops

Ingredients:

- **8 lamb chops**
- **2 tablespoons olive oil**
- **2 cloves garlic**, minced
- **1 tablespoon fresh rosemary**, chopped
- **Salt and pepper** (to taste)

Instructions:

1. Preheat grill to medium-high heat.
2. Rub the lamb chops with olive oil, garlic, rosemary, salt, and pepper.
3. Grill the lamb chops for 4-5 minutes on each side for medium-rare, or longer for desired doneness.
4. Let the lamb chops rest for a few minutes before serving.

Sweet Potato Fries

Ingredients:

- **2 large sweet potatoes**, peeled and cut into fries
- **2 tablespoons olive oil**
- **1 teaspoon paprika**
- **Salt and pepper** (to taste)

Instructions:

1. Preheat grill to medium-high heat.
2. Toss the sweet potato fries in olive oil, paprika, salt, and pepper.
3. Grill the fries for 10-12 minutes, turning occasionally, until crispy and tender.
4. Serve hot with a dipping sauce of your choice.

Grilled Flatbreads with Toppings

Ingredients:

- **2 store-bought or homemade flatbreads**
- **Olive oil**, for brushing
- **1/2 cup hummus** (optional)
- **1/2 cup crumbled feta cheese**
- **1/2 cup sliced cherry tomatoes**
- **1/4 cup fresh basil**, chopped
- **Salt and pepper** (to taste)

Instructions:

1. Preheat grill to medium-high heat.
2. Brush the flatbreads with olive oil and grill for 2-3 minutes per side until slightly charred.
3. Remove from the grill and spread with hummus if using.
4. Top with feta, cherry tomatoes, basil, salt, and pepper.
5. Serve warm.

BBQ Chicken Caesar Salad

Ingredients:

- **4 boneless, skinless chicken breasts**
- **1 tablespoon olive oil**
- **Salt and pepper** (to taste)
- **6 cups Romaine lettuce**, chopped
- **1/4 cup Caesar dressing**
- **1/4 cup Parmesan cheese**, grated
- **Croutons** (optional)

Instructions:

1. Preheat grill to medium-high heat.
2. Season the chicken breasts with olive oil, salt, and pepper.
3. Grill the chicken for 6-7 minutes on each side until fully cooked.
4. Let the chicken rest for a few minutes before slicing.
5. Toss Romaine lettuce with Caesar dressing and top with sliced chicken, Parmesan cheese, and croutons.
6. Serve immediately.

Grilled Beef Tenderloin

Ingredients:

- **1.5 lbs beef tenderloin**, trimmed
- **2 tablespoons olive oil**
- **2 cloves garlic**, minced
- **1 tablespoon fresh rosemary**, chopped
- **1 tablespoon fresh thyme**, chopped
- **Salt and pepper** (to taste)

Instructions:

1. Preheat grill to medium-high heat.
2. Rub the beef tenderloin with olive oil, garlic, rosemary, thyme, salt, and pepper.
3. Grill the tenderloin for 4-6 minutes per side, or until it reaches your desired level of doneness.
4. Let the beef rest for 10 minutes before slicing and serving.

Roasted Garlic and Herb Chicken

Ingredients:

- **4 bone-in, skin-on chicken thighs**
- **2 tablespoons olive oil**
- **4 cloves garlic**, minced
- **1 tablespoon fresh thyme**, chopped
- **1 tablespoon fresh rosemary**, chopped
- **Salt and pepper** (to taste)

Instructions:

1. Preheat grill to medium heat.
2. Rub the chicken thighs with olive oil, garlic, thyme, rosemary, salt, and pepper.
3. Grill the chicken for 7-8 minutes per side, or until the internal temperature reaches 165°F (75°C).
4. Serve hot with your favorite side dish.

BBQ Duck Breast

Ingredients:

- **4 duck breasts**
- **2 tablespoons olive oil**
- **Salt and pepper** (to taste)
- **1/2 cup BBQ sauce**

Instructions:

1. Preheat grill to medium-high heat.
2. Score the skin of the duck breasts in a crisscross pattern, then rub with olive oil, salt, and pepper.
3. Grill the duck breasts, skin-side down, for 6-8 minutes, then flip and grill for an additional 4-5 minutes.
4. Brush the duck breasts with BBQ sauce during the last few minutes of grilling.
5. Rest the duck for a few minutes before serving.

Grilled Caprese Skewers

Ingredients:

- **1 pint cherry tomatoes**
- **1 ball fresh mozzarella**, cut into cubes
- **Fresh basil leaves**
- **2 tablespoons balsamic glaze**
- **Olive oil** (for brushing)
- **Salt and pepper** (to taste)
- **Wooden skewers** (soaked in water for 30 minutes)

Instructions:

1. Preheat grill to medium heat.
2. Thread the cherry tomatoes, mozzarella cubes, and basil leaves onto the skewers.
3. Brush the skewers with olive oil and season with salt and pepper.
4. Grill the skewers for 2-3 minutes, turning occasionally, until the mozzarella is slightly melted.
5. Drizzle with balsamic glaze before serving.

Sweet BBQ Glazed Baby Carrots

Ingredients:

- 1 lb baby carrots
- 2 tablespoons olive oil
- 1/4 cup BBQ sauce
- 1 tablespoon honey
- **Salt and pepper** (to taste)

Instructions:

1. Preheat grill to medium heat.
2. Toss the baby carrots in olive oil, salt, and pepper.
3. Grill the carrots for 10-12 minutes, turning occasionally, until tender and slightly charred.
4. In a small bowl, combine BBQ sauce and honey.
5. Brush the carrots with the BBQ glaze during the last 2-3 minutes of grilling.
6. Serve hot.

BBQ Sliced Brisket Tacos

Ingredients:

- 2 lbs beef brisket
- 2 tablespoons olive oil
- 1/4 cup BBQ rub
- 1 cup BBQ sauce
- 8 small soft corn tortillas
- **Coleslaw** (optional topping)
- **Pickled onions** (optional topping)

Instructions:

1. Preheat grill to medium heat.
2. Rub the brisket with olive oil and BBQ rub.
3. Grill the brisket for 5-6 hours, indirect cooking, until it reaches an internal temperature of 200°F (93°C).
4. Rest the brisket for 10-15 minutes before slicing thinly against the grain.
5. Serve the brisket on tortillas with BBQ sauce, coleslaw, and pickled onions.

Grilled Bacon-Wrapped Jalapeños

Ingredients:

- **8 large jalapeños**, halved and seeded
- **8 ounces cream cheese**, softened
- **1/4 cup shredded cheddar cheese**
- **8 slices bacon**
- **Toothpicks** (for securing)

Instructions:

1. Preheat grill to medium-high heat.
2. In a bowl, mix cream cheese and cheddar cheese.
3. Stuff each jalapeño half with the cheese mixture.
4. Wrap each stuffed jalapeño with a slice of bacon and secure with toothpicks.
5. Grill the jalapeños for 5-7 minutes per side until the bacon is crispy and the peppers are tender.
6. Serve hot.

BBQ Veggie Skewers

Ingredients:

- **1 zucchini**, sliced into thick rounds
- **1 red bell pepper**, cut into chunks
- **1 yellow bell pepper**, cut into chunks
- **1 red onion**, cut into chunks
- **8 oz mushrooms**, whole or halved
- **2 tablespoons olive oil**
- **Salt and pepper** (to taste)
- **1 tablespoon balsamic vinegar**

Instructions:

1. Preheat grill to medium-high heat.
2. Thread the vegetables onto skewers, alternating between zucchini, peppers, onion, and mushrooms.
3. Brush the skewers with olive oil and season with salt and pepper.
4. Grill the veggie skewers for 4-5 minutes per side, until charred and tender.
5. Drizzle with balsamic vinegar before serving.

Grilled Flat Iron Steak

Ingredients:

- **1.5 lbs flat iron steak**
- **2 tablespoons olive oil**
- **2 cloves garlic**, minced
- **1 tablespoon fresh rosemary**, chopped
- **Salt and pepper** (to taste)

Instructions:

1. Preheat grill to high heat.
2. Rub the steak with olive oil, garlic, rosemary, salt, and pepper.
3. Grill the flat iron steak for 4-6 minutes per side, or until it reaches your desired doneness.
4. Rest the steak for 5-10 minutes before slicing against the grain and serving.

Roasted Corn and Black Bean Salad

Ingredients:

- **4 ears corn**, husked
- **1 can (15 oz) black beans**, drained and rinsed
- **1 red bell pepper**, diced
- **1/2 red onion**, finely chopped
- **1/4 cup fresh cilantro**, chopped
- **2 tablespoons olive oil**
- **1 tablespoon lime juice**
- **Salt and pepper** (to taste)

Instructions:

1. Preheat grill to medium-high heat.
2. Grill the corn for about 10 minutes, turning occasionally until charred.
3. Let the corn cool, then cut the kernels off the cob.
4. In a bowl, mix the grilled corn, black beans, red bell pepper, onion, and cilantro.
5. Drizzle with olive oil and lime juice, and season with salt and pepper. Toss to combine and serve.

BBQ Beef Short Ribs

Ingredients:

- 3 lbs beef short ribs
- 2 tablespoons olive oil
- 1/4 cup BBQ rub
- 1 cup BBQ sauce

Instructions:

1. Preheat grill to medium heat.
2. Rub the short ribs with olive oil and BBQ rub.
3. Grill the ribs over indirect heat for 3-4 hours, turning occasionally.
4. In the last 30 minutes, brush with BBQ sauce every 10 minutes.
5. Let the ribs rest for 10 minutes before serving.

Grilled Fajita Veggies

Ingredients:

- **1 red bell pepper**, sliced
- **1 yellow bell pepper**, sliced
- **1 red onion**, sliced
- **2 tablespoons olive oil**
- **1 teaspoon cumin**
- **1 teaspoon paprika**
- **Salt and pepper** (to taste)

Instructions:

1. Preheat grill to medium heat.
2. Toss the peppers and onion in olive oil, cumin, paprika, salt, and pepper.
3. Grill the veggies in a grill basket or on skewers for about 8-10 minutes, turning occasionally, until tender and charred.
4. Serve as a side dish or with grilled fajitas.

BBQ Sausage and Peppers Sandwiches

Ingredients:

- **4 sausages** (such as Italian or bratwurst)
- **2 bell peppers**, sliced
- **1 onion**, sliced
- **1 tablespoon olive oil**
- **Salt and pepper** (to taste)
- **4 sandwich buns**

Instructions:

1. Preheat grill to medium heat.
2. Grill the sausages for about 8-10 minutes, turning occasionally, until fully cooked.
3. In a grill-safe pan, sauté the peppers and onion with olive oil, salt, and pepper, until tender and charred.
4. Serve the sausages on buns, topped with the grilled peppers and onions.

Grilled Avocados with Salsa

Ingredients:

- **4 ripe avocados**, halved and pitted
- **1 tablespoon olive oil**
- **Salt and pepper** (to taste)
- **1 cup fresh salsa** (store-bought or homemade)

Instructions:

1. Preheat grill to medium heat.
2. Brush the avocado halves with olive oil, and season with salt and pepper.
3. Grill the avocados cut-side down for 3-4 minutes until grill marks appear.
4. Top with fresh salsa and serve.

BBQ Grilled Chicken Wraps

Ingredients:

- **4 boneless, skinless chicken breasts**
- **1/4 cup BBQ sauce**
- **4 large flour tortillas**
- **1 cup shredded lettuce**
- **1/2 cup shredded cheese** (cheddar or mozzarella)
- **1/4 cup diced tomatoes**

Instructions:

1. Preheat grill to medium-high heat.
2. Grill the chicken breasts for 6-7 minutes per side until fully cooked.
3. Brush with BBQ sauce during the last 2 minutes of grilling.
4. Slice the chicken and assemble the wraps by placing the chicken, lettuce, cheese, and tomatoes in each tortilla.
5. Roll up and serve.

Grilled Clams with Garlic Butter

Ingredients:

- **2 dozen fresh clams**, scrubbed
- **1/2 cup unsalted butter**, melted
- **3 cloves garlic**, minced
- **1 tablespoon fresh parsley**, chopped
- **Lemon wedges** (for serving)

Instructions:

1. Preheat grill to medium heat.
2. Place the clams directly on the grill grates and cook for 5-7 minutes, until the shells open.
3. In a bowl, mix melted butter, garlic, and parsley.
4. Remove the clams from the grill and drizzle with garlic butter.
5. Serve with lemon wedges.

BBQ Smoked Sausages with Sauerkraut

Ingredients:

- **4 smoked sausages**
- **2 cups sauerkraut**, drained
- **1 tablespoon olive oil**
- **1 teaspoon caraway seeds**
- **Salt and pepper** (to taste)

Instructions:

1. Preheat grill to medium heat.
2. Grill the sausages for about 8-10 minutes, turning occasionally, until browned and heated through.
3. While grilling the sausages, heat sauerkraut in a pan over medium heat with olive oil, caraway seeds, salt, and pepper.
4. Serve the sausages topped with sauerkraut.

Grilled BBQ Sliders

Ingredients:

- 1 lb ground beef
- 1/4 cup BBQ sauce
- **Salt and pepper** (to taste)
- 4 slider buns
- **1/2 cup shredded cheese** (cheddar or American)
- **Pickles** (optional)

Instructions:

1. Preheat grill to medium-high heat.
2. Form the ground beef into 4 small patties, season with salt and pepper.
3. Grill the patties for 3-4 minutes per side, brushing with BBQ sauce during the last minute of grilling.
4. Toast the buns on the grill for 1-2 minutes.
5. Assemble the sliders by placing the cooked patties on the buns, adding cheese, and optional pickles.
6. Serve immediately.

BBQ Grilled Fish Fillets

Ingredients:

- **4 fish fillets** (such as tilapia, cod, or salmon)
- **2 tablespoons olive oil**
- **1 tablespoon lemon juice**
- **1 teaspoon smoked paprika**
- **Salt and pepper** (to taste)

Instructions:

1. Preheat grill to medium heat.
2. Brush the fish fillets with olive oil, lemon juice, smoked paprika, salt, and pepper.
3. Grill the fish for 3-4 minutes per side, until cooked through and flaky.
4. Serve with additional lemon wedges or your favorite dipping sauce.

Grilled Stuffed Bell Peppers

Ingredients:

- **4 large bell peppers**, tops cut off and seeds removed
- **1 cup cooked rice**
- **1/2 lb ground beef or turkey**
- **1/2 cup shredded cheese** (cheddar or mozzarella)
- **1/4 cup diced onion**
- **1/4 cup diced tomatoes**
- **1 tablespoon olive oil**
- **Salt and pepper** (to taste)

Instructions:

1. Preheat grill to medium heat.
2. In a pan, cook the ground beef or turkey with onion until browned. Stir in cooked rice, tomatoes, and salt and pepper.
3. Stuff the bell peppers with the beef and rice mixture.
4. Brush the peppers with olive oil and season with salt and pepper.
5. Grill the peppers on the grill for 15-20 minutes, or until the peppers are tender and the filling is heated through.
6. Top with cheese during the last 5 minutes of grilling.

BBQ Brisket Nachos

Ingredients:

- **1 lb leftover BBQ brisket**, shredded
- **Tortilla chips**
- **1 cup shredded cheese** (cheddar or Monterey Jack)
- **1/2 cup sour cream**
- **1/4 cup jalapeños**, sliced
- **1/4 cup green onions**, chopped
- **BBQ sauce** (optional)

Instructions:

1. Preheat grill to medium heat.
2. On a grill-safe pan, spread tortilla chips evenly.
3. Top with shredded brisket and cheese.
4. Grill for 5-7 minutes until the cheese is melted and bubbly.
5. Remove from grill and top with sour cream, jalapeños, green onions, and drizzle with extra BBQ sauce if desired.
6. Serve immediately.

Grilled Eggplant with Tahini Sauce

Ingredients:

- **2 medium eggplants**, sliced into 1-inch rounds
- **2 tablespoons olive oil**
- **Salt and pepper** (to taste)
- **1/4 cup tahini**
- **1 tablespoon lemon juice**
- **1 clove garlic**, minced
- **1 tablespoon water** (to thin the sauce)

Instructions:

1. Preheat grill to medium heat.
2. Brush the eggplant slices with olive oil and season with salt and pepper.
3. Grill the eggplant for 3-4 minutes per side until tender and grill marks appear.
4. In a bowl, whisk together tahini, lemon juice, garlic, and water until smooth.
5. Drizzle the tahini sauce over the grilled eggplant and serve.

Grilled BBQ Chicken Pizza

Ingredients:

- **1 pizza dough** (store-bought or homemade)
- **1/2 cup BBQ sauce**
- **1 lb cooked chicken breast**, shredded
- **1/2 cup red onion**, thinly sliced
- **1 cup shredded mozzarella cheese**
- **1/2 cup shredded cheddar cheese**
- **Cilantro leaves** (optional)

Instructions:

1. Preheat grill to medium heat.
2. Roll out the pizza dough to your desired size.
3. Grill the dough on one side for 2-3 minutes, then flip.
4. Brush the grilled side with BBQ sauce and top with shredded chicken, red onion, and both cheeses.
5. Grill the pizza for another 4-5 minutes until the cheese is melted and bubbly.
6. Remove from the grill and sprinkle with cilantro leaves before serving.

Grilled Watermelon with Mint

Ingredients:

- **1 small watermelon**, cut into wedges
- **1 tablespoon olive oil**
- **Salt** (to taste)
- **1 tablespoon fresh mint**, chopped
- **1 teaspoon lime juice**

Instructions:

1. Preheat grill to medium heat.
2. Brush the watermelon wedges with olive oil and season with a pinch of salt.
3. Grill the watermelon for 2-3 minutes per side, until grill marks appear and the watermelon is slightly caramelized.
4. Remove from the grill and drizzle with lime juice, and sprinkle with chopped mint.
5. Serve immediately.